Geothermal
Energy

# Geothermal Energy

Christopher Bahn



CREATIVE EDUCATION
CREATIVE PAPERBACKS

Published by Creative Education and Creative Paperbacks
P.O. Box 227, Mankato, Minnesota 56002
Creative Education and Creative Paperbacks are imprints
of The Creative Company
www.thecreativecompany.us

Book design by Blue Design (www.bluedes.com)
Art direction by Graham Morgan
Edited by Barbara Ciletti

Photographs by Getty Images/Dominika Zarzycka/NurPhoto,
17, Heritage Images, 19, JEREMIE RICHARD, 34, John Malmin,
20, Mint Images, 30, Patrick Meinhardt/Bloomberg, 41, Tina
Zupancic, 14; Pexels/Gylfi Gylfason, 45, Maria Christensen,
cover, Tyler Lastovich, 37,  Lady Sponge, 4–5; Shutterstock/
VectorMine, 13; Unsplash/Dan Meyers, 36, Jacques Dillies, 9,
Kameron Kincade, 2, Nina Luong, 25, Sam Bark, 26; Wikimedia
Commons/Carleton Watkins, 23, Gretar Ívarsson - Edited by
Fir0002, cover, 10, Julien Carnot, 29, Lydur Skulason, 6–7, Mark
Johnson, 44, Paul Gipe, 33



Library of Congress Cataloging-in-Publication Data
Names: Bahn, Christopher (Children's story writer) author
Title: Geothermal energy / by Christopher Bahn.
Description: Mankato, Minnesota : Creative Education and
  Creative  Paperbacks, [2026] | Series: Living in the future |
  Includes bibliographical references and index. | Audience:
  Ages 10-14. |  Audience: Grades 7-9. | Summary: "Readers
  learn about harnessing Earth's natural heat for power. It
  explains the process and applications of geothermal systems
  as an eco-friendly energy solution for the future. Written for
  middle-grade readers, it includes real-life examples of
  energy use, sidebars, a glossary, and an index"-- Provided by
  publisher.
Identifiers: LCCN 2025015996 (print) | LCCN 2025015997 (ebook)
  | ISBN 9798895811214 library binding | ISBN 9798896800743
  paperback | ISBN 9798895812471 ebook
Subjects: LCSH: Geothermal power plants--Juvenile literature
  | Geothermal resources--Juvenile literature | Geothermal
  engineering--Juvenile  literature
Classification: LCC TK1055 .B34 2026  (print) | LCC TK1055
  (ebook) | DDC 333.8/8--dc23/eng/20250904
LC record available at https://lccn.loc.gov/2025015996
LC ebook record available at https://lccn.loc.gov/2025015997

Printed in the United States

# CONTENTS

# Power from the Earth

There is an ancient, titanic fire burning beneath your feet, so big that it makes up almost the entirety of the Earth itself. Sometimes, this mass of boiling lava breaks through to the surface, and can cause incredible destruction through earthquakes and volcanoes. Like Mount Vesuvius, which famously buried the Roman city of Pompeii under tons of ash and rock in the eruption of 79 C.E. Another eruption, at Mount Toba in Indonesia 74,000 years ago, was so cataclysmic that it nearly caused the extinction of the entire human species!

But that awesome force can also be harnessed for good. The same churning heat that destroyed Pompeii also brings life and prosperity to people all over the world—in the form of **geothermal** power. Geothermal, meaning "heat from the Earth," draws on the superheated rocks deep below the surface for our civilization's energy needs. It takes some work to get to it, but geothermal has almost limitless potential—and could help us transition away from dangerous, climate-altering **fossil fuels** into a future dominated by renewable energy sources like solar, wind, and hydropower.

Unlike coal or gas plants, geothermal power plants don't burn fuel—they generate power using Earth's natural heat.

# CHAPTER 1

# How it Works

Energy is central to human civilization. Modern society requires large amounts of energy to function, and we have built enormous, complex systems to generate and distribute that energy.

Continent-spanning networks of power lines connect our cities, homes, hospitals, and schools. Thousands of miles of roads carry millions of cars and trucks. Trains, airplanes and cargo ships criss-cross the world. Our energy network runs largely on fossil fuels such as coal, oil, and gas. But these fuels are expensive, polluting, and contribute to **global warming**—and they will eventually be used up. It is increasingly important to find **renewable** and **sustainable** alternative energy sources, including solar, wind, hydropower, nuclear power, biofuels, and the topic of this book, geothermal energy.

Geothermal energy comes from the heat deep inside the Earth. This heat can be used to warm buildings and generate electricity. If we could fully tap into this heat, it could power the world for millions of years. But it isn't always easy to reach. Setting up geothermal wells takes a lot of time, money, and effort. Right now, geothermal energy makes up only about 0.4% of the world's energy. However, new technology could change that. In the right places, geothermal power is a clean, reliable, and efficient source of energy.

The Earth was once a ball of molten rock when it formed 4.5 billion years ago. Over time, it cooled enough for a solid surface to form. Deep inside, the Earth stays extremely hot. This heat comes from leftover energy from when the planet formed and from radioactive elements like uranium and thorium that release heat as they break down.

Scientists study the Earth's interior using earthquake waves. These waves move through the planet at different speeds depending on the material they pass through. This helps scientists understand Earth's layers.

The outer layer, called the crust, is the coolest and thinnest, ranging from 3 to 43 miles (5 to 70 kilometers) thick. Below that is the mantle, about 1,800 mi (2,900 km) thick, where some rock gets hot enough to melt. The core, made of iron and nickel, is divided into two parts. The inner core is solid, about 758 mi (1,220 km) thick, and reaches temperatures of 9,800° Fahrenheit (5,400°Celsius)—as hot as the sun's surface. The outer core is liquid and helps create Earth's magnetic field.

# GEOTHERMAL ENERGY

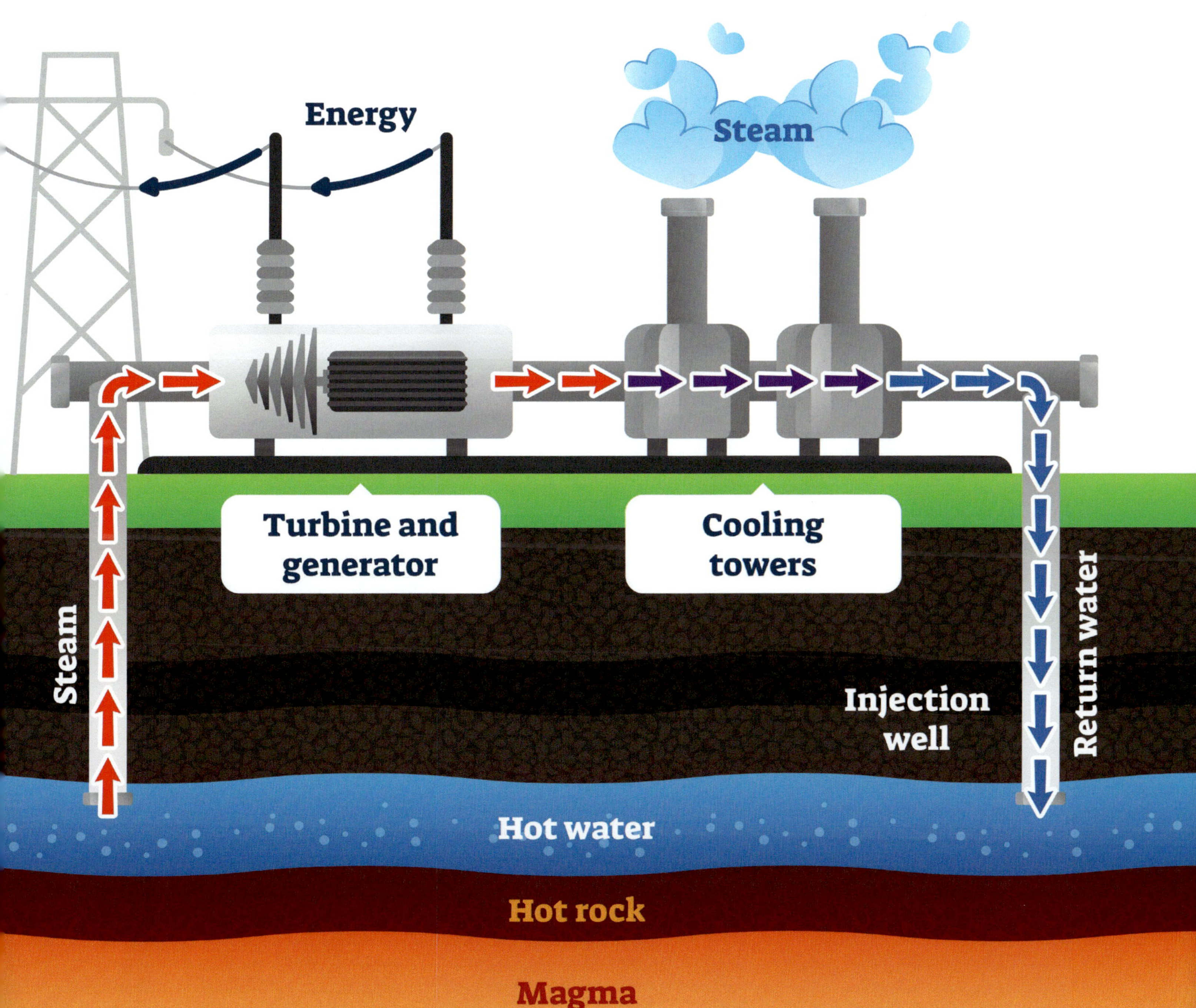

## ZOOM IN: SLIP SLIDING AWAY

The reason that earthquakes and volcanoes exist is explained by the concept of plate tectonics. Geologists have found that the Earth's crust is broken up into several dozen immense tectonic plates, which make up our continents and ocean basins. These plates are constantly moving, pulling apart or colliding into one another in a process known as continental drift. They move very slowly, inches per year on average, but over time the movement of the plates raises mountains, creates earthquakes, and completely reshapes the layout of the continents. The fracture zones and collision boundaries between plates form a web around the whole world.

In some places, heat from inside the Earth rises close to the surface, creating hot springs, geysers, and volcanoes. These areas, found near tectonic plate boundaries or volcanic hot spots like Yellowstone or Hawaii, are great for geothermal energy. While geothermal energy can be produced anywhere with deep drilling, it is easiest to use in these high-heat regions. Unlike solar or wind power, geothermal energy is not affected by the weather—it's available all the time.

Geothermal energy can heat homes, greenhouses, factories, and even swimming pools. It is also used to generate electricity for cities and entire countries. Some places, like Iceland, California, Italy, and New Zealand, have strong geothermal resources. Large geothermal power plants drill deep underground—about 0.6 mi (1 km)—to reach hot, water-filled rocks. The hot water turns into steam, which spins turbines to produce electricity. If the water runs out, more can be pumped in to keep the system working.

Geothermal energy can also work on a smaller scale. Ground-source heat pumps don't need to drill deep. They take advantage of the steady underground temperature just 30 to 50 ft (10 to 15 m) below the surface to heat or cool buildings.

This energy source has great potential. In Southeast Asia, geothermal, solar, and hydropower are cheaper than coal. Kenya has also made big changes, with over 80% of its electricity coming from renewables like wind, solar, and geothermal power. Iceland, which

Thingvellir National Park, located in Selfoss, Iceland, is where the Eurasian and North American tectonic plates meet.

gets nearly all of its electricity from hydropower and geothermal, has almost no **greenhouse gas** emissions from power generation.

Despite this, geothermal energy has been slow to expand. It is expensive to build new wells, and drilling deep into the Earth can sometimes cause small earthquakes, similar to **fracking** in the oil industry. But once a geothermal plant is built, it is clean, steady, and affordable to run. Currently, geothermal energy provides only a tiny fraction of the world's power—about 0.25%. However, some experts predict it could grow to 3% by 2050. The U.S. alone could get up to 25% of its energy from geothermal if the right investments are made.

While solar and wind will likely remain the main sources of renewable energy, geothermal can play an important role in the clean energy mix. It is reliable, sustainable, and has the potential to power the future.



Except in the rare instance when a volcanic vent or hot spring brings heat naturally to the surface, geothermal power requires drilling wells deep underground. It's not unlike drilling for oil, and needs the same kind of expertise. But there are significant differences. One is scale: Geothermal wells must go much deeper to reach hot rock, and often cover an area of 2,000 meters or more, whereas oil wells generally pinpoint one location. Most oil wells are also short-term projects, exhausting themselves in 10 to 15 years. But geothermal wells can last for generations, and must be built to last.

A large geothermal drill site in Poland.

# CHAPTER 2

# A History of Geothermal Power

Geothermal energy has been around as long as the Earth itself, and people have been using it for thousands of years. Ancient humans often lived in caves partly because underground temperatures stay warm and steady. Native American tribes gathered at what is now Hot Springs National Park in Arkansas 10,000 years ago, treating it as a peaceful and spiritual place.

Many ancient civilizations, including those in China, Japan, Greece, and Rome, used hot springs and geysers for bathing and heating water. The ancient Greeks believed that volcanoes were connected to their gods. Poseidon, the god of earthquakes, was seen as a force of destruction, while Hephaestus, the blacksmith god, was thought to have his fiery workshop inside a volcano. Some versions of the myth of Prometheus say that when he stole fire from the gods for

The Romans utilized geothermal energy in their extravagent bath houses.

Unlike Jules Verne's fiction, reaching Earth's center is no easy feat. Russia's Kola Superdeep Borehole holds the record for the deepest manmade hole, reaching 12.2 kilometers (7.6 miles) in 1990—still far from the mantle. In 1961, the U.S. attempted oceanic drilling with Project Mohole but only hit 183 meters (601 feet). The Deep Sea Drilling Project later pushed to 1,741 meters (5,712 feet). Meanwhile, Norway's Ryfast tunnel, the deepest in regular use, descends 292 meters (958 feet) below sea level, connecting the cities of Stavanger and Strand.

Project Mohole used sections of pipe that were lowered into the sea from a vessel.

humans, it came from Hephaestus' forge—making it one of the earliest geothermal stories. The city of Bath, England, was built by the Romans in 60 C.E. because of its hot springs. It remained an important religious and healing site for centuries, with even the legendary King Arthur linked to battles near the area.

People have traditionally used geothermal energy in places with natural volcanic vents or faults, like Iceland, California, Italy, and New Zealand. In Iceland, 9 out of 10 homes are heated with geothermal energy. Even in freezing weather, the temperature just 6 meters (20 feet) below the surface is warm enough to heat buildings. Some towns use district heating, where a system carries geothermal heat to multiple homes. This idea is very old—the village of Chaudes-Aigues in France has used hot springs for heating since 1332. Wooden pipes carried heat to houses then, and today the system still warms over 100 homes.

The western U.S. has many geothermal sources, including the massive supervolcano beneath Yellowstone National Park. Though it hasn't erupted in 70,000 years, Yellowstone remains geologically active and has over half of the world's geysers. To protect the park, geothermal plants are not allowed there. However, nearby areas have played a big role in developing geothermal energy for nearly 200 years. In 1830, Asa Thompson in Hot Springs, Arkansas, charged people $1 to bathe in spring-fed wooden tubs—one of the first known commercial uses of geothermal energy. A larger example was the Hot Lake Hotel in Oregon, built in 1864. The hotel, known for its "healing waters," was the first large building heated by geothermal energy.

Geothermal power moved into the modern age in the early 1900s. Italian prince Piero Conti was the first to show that geothermal energy could make electricity. In 1904, at his palace in Larderello, he powered four lightbulbs using a steam-driven generator. While a small step, it proved the idea worked. In 1911, Conti built a geothermal power plant that generated 250 kilowatts of electricity. That plant has since grown into the world's second-largest geothermal power complex, producing around 750 megawatts today. The next large-scale geothermal plant wasn't built until 1958 in Wairakei, New Zealand.

A small California resort town called The Geysers became a major site for geothermal power. For thousands of years, Native American tribes held ceremonies there. In 1852, it became a resort, visited by famous people like Ulysses S. Grant, Theodore Roosevelt, and Mark Twain. The first American geothermal power plant was built there in 1922, producing electricity for the resort. In 1960, Pacific Gas and Electric built the U.S.'s first large geothermal power plant at The Geysers. Today, it is the largest geothermal plant in the world, producing more than twice the power of Larderello.

The Geysers in 1868

In 1927, the Pioneer Development Company drilled exploratory wells in Imperial Valley, California, looking for underground steam. They didn't find the right conditions, but they were onto something—today, the area is home to the Imperial Valley Geothermal Project, the second-largest geothermal plant in the U.S.

The 1970s energy crisis forced many countries to look for alternatives to oil. At the same time, scientists were learning more about climate change and the dangers of fossil fuels. This led to government-sponsored research on alternative energy, including geothermal. Research continued in the 1990s and 2000s, improving geothermal technology for both electricity generation and home heating.

For centuries, people used geothermal heat to warm buildings, but the idea didn't spread widely until the 20th century. Boise, Idaho, was the first modern city to create a geothermal district heating system, starting on Warm Springs Avenue. Today, the city has a 20-mile **pipeline**



Geothermal technology has revolutionized food production, enabling year-round farming in cold climates. Edwards Greenhouse in Boise pioneered large-scale geothermal greenhouses in 1930. Today, it's used in food dehydration, fish farming, and various agricultural processes. Italian farmers harness geothermal heat to brew beer, make pecorino cheese, and grow produce. In California's Imperial Valley, geofarms raise over a million tons of fish—and even alligators. New Zealand's Upflow advances sustainable geothermal farming by recycling greenhouse carbon dioxide, reducing reliance on fossil fuels.

system that heats over 6 million square feet of buildings—the largest in the U.S. Other cities, like Klamath Falls, Oregon, have also built geothermal heating systems. In 1948, Ohio State University professor Carl Nielsen invented a smaller version of this technology, the ground-source heat pump, which he used to heat his own home.

# Geothermal Today

Geothermal power has grown a lot in the last 50 years. In 2023, the world produced eight times more geothermal energy than in 1980. The United States was the first country to use geothermal power in a big way and is still the world leader. But compared to other energy sources like solar, wind, and fossil fuels, geothermal makes up only a small part of America's electricity.

The U.S. Energy Information Administration estimated that in 2023, geothermal energy made about 16,000 gigawatt-hours of electricity— less than half a percent of the 4 million gigawatt-hours produced by all energy sources.

The top eight countries with the most geothermal energy in 2023 were the U.S., Indonesia, Turkey, New Zealand, Mexico, Kenya, Italy, and Iceland. These countries have a lot of volcanic activity, which creates underground heat. Iceland, in particular, uses a huge

Geothermal plants run 24/7, producing stable power without the noise and emissions of traditional power stations.

amount of geothermal energy. But Iceland is unique because it sits right on top of one of the world's largest volcanic rifts. Most countries don't have such an easy-to-use geothermal resource.

Geothermal power is used in two main ways. Small-scale systems, like heat pumps, provide energy for homes or neighborhoods. Large-scale geothermal plants generate electricity for entire regions. These big plants drill into underground heat reservoirs, similar to how oil wells are drilled. However, geothermal wells are often larger and contain hot, mineral-rich fluids that can be corrosive, making it hard to reuse old oil wells for geothermal power.

There are three main types of geothermal power plants: dry steam, flash steam, and binary. They all work in a similar way— heat from underground turns water into steam, which spins a

A geothermal plant in Iceland. Turbines create electricity for the region from a nearby volcanic hotspot.

turbine connected to a generator to produce electricity. In some cases, the water exists naturally in underground reservoirs. Other times, water is injected underground, similar to fracking in oil fields. Water is an excellent way to transfer heat, but underground water isn't always clean. It often contains minerals, gases, and even heavy metals that can be harmful if they leak into surface water.

Geothermal power works best on a large scale. Geothermal plants are safer and more sustainable than fossil fuel plants, but working with these superhot, sometimes corrosive fluids can be dangerous. Once a geothermal plant is built, it is relatively cheap to run. However, drilling deep enough to reach the heat source can be expensive. The cost also depends on the flow rate of the underground fluid, which is affected by natural pressure.

Dry steam power plants use underground reservoirs of superhot steam, with no liquid water present. These systems work by drilling two wells: one to bring up steam and another to inject cooler water back down. The wells must be far enough apart so they don't interfere with each other. Since reservoirs of dry steam have low pressure, pumps are needed. Dry steam technology is the oldest and simplest type of geothermal power. It was first used in Italy in 1904 and later at The Geysers in California.

Flash steam power plants pull up very hot water from a high-pressure underground reservoir and release it into a low-pressure tank. This sudden drop in pressure causes the water to instantly turn into steam, which spins a turbine. These wells must be extremely hot—around 360°F (180°C) or more—making them more difficult and expensive to build. The best locations for flash steam plants have a steady supply of underground water at high temperatures. Sometimes, the steam is used in multiple turbines to generate extra power before being cooled and reinjected underground.

**B**inary power plants are the newest geothermal technology. They use moderately hot water, below 400°F, or even cooler. Instead of turning to steam, the hot water passes through a heat exchanger, which transfers the heat to a second liquid (such as pentane or butane) that boils at a lower temperature. This vapor then spins a turbine. Binary plants currently make up about 15% of geothermal power plants, but their popularity is growing. They are more efficient than flash steam plants and cause almost no pollution. Because they use cooler underground fluids, they can be built in many more places than older geothermal plants.

Mammoth Geothermal Complex in California is a binary power plant.

The Blue Lagoon in Iceland

Geothermal energy isn't just for making electricity. It can heat homes and entire neighborhoods, melt ice on roads and sidewalks, and warm water for fish farms and greenhouses. As of 2022, nearly 400 geothermal district heating systems were operating in Europe. Farmers use geothermal energy to pasteurize milk, dry fruits and vegetables, and heat soil for crops. A well-designed system can even reuse its heat for multiple purposes. For example, the same geothermal energy can first generate electricity, then heat buildings, and finally be used in agriculture.

# CHAPTER 4

# The Future of Geothermal

**G**eothermal energy production grew by 30% from 2000 to 2022. That sounds impressive, but other renewable energy sources grew even faster—by 116% in the same period.

Right now, geothermal energy makes up only about 14 gigawatts of the world's electricity—less than 1% of the total, including fossil fuels. Paul F. Meier, author of *The Changing Energy Mix*, believes geothermal power could eventually reach 211 gigawatts. However, it hasn't expanded as quickly as many had hoped.

The U.S. Energy Information Administration highlights several challenges in expanding geothermal energy. Many geothermal sites are located in remote areas, making it difficult to build power plants and transmit electricity to cities. Construction is also a lengthy process, often taking up to eight years—far longer than

High temperatures in geothermal hot spots cause minerals to dissolve and react, forming vibrant colors in hot springs and mud pools.

## ZOOM IN: ANCHORING EARTHSHIPS

The dwarves and hobbits of *Lord of the Rings* thrived underground—maybe they were onto something. Subterranean homes, like "earthships," are eco-friendly, self-sustaining structures designed to minimize reliance on outside power. Built partly underground, they harness stable temperatures to cut heating and cooling costs. Though still experimental, earthships offer a unique, if challenging, way to live like Bilbo Baggins.

solar or wind farms. Environmental concerns add complexity, requiring careful measures to prevent water pollution and protect underground heat reservoirs. While advanced geothermal technology could unlock deeper heat sources, the high costs remain a barrier to widespread use.

**D**espite these obstacles, geothermal power remains a reliable and clean energy source with significant potential. It could even contribute to space exploration by harnessing underground heat on other planets and moons—though "geothermal" might not be the right term for such extraterrestrial applications. Perhaps "Mars-o-thermal" would be more fitting. In some places, geothermal energy already makes a huge impact. Tuscany, Italy, gets 30% of its electricity from it, while Kenya relies on it for about 50%. In the U.S., over 90% of geothermal power comes from California and Nevada. The best future sites are in the western states, including Alaska and Hawaii, where there is more volcanic activity. Meier predicts major growth in places like Indonesia, Japan, and Chile, which are part of the Pacific Ocean's "Ring of Fire," an area known for volcanoes and earthquakes. Other places also show promise, such as Poland's Carpathian Mountains and

France, which already heats many homes using a geothermal basin under Paris. Mongolia, famous for its hot springs, may also become a key player in geothermal power.

Kenya is a leader in geothermal energy. The country's Olkaria Geothermal Power Station generates nearly 900 megawatts of power, and Kenya hopes to increase that by five times by 2030. It is also working to help other countries in East Africa, like Ethiopia, develop their own geothermal energy. Ethiopia has similar volcanic resources and could benefit just as much as Kenya has.

What does the future hold for geothermal energy? Bruce Usher, author of *Renewable Energy: A Primer for the Twenty-first Century*, believes geothermal has limited potential because the easiest-to-access sites are already in use. Others disagree. The University of Michigan's Center for Sustainable Systems is optimistic, stating that while the U.S. currently uses less than 1% of its geothermal potential, new technology could allow access to nearly all of it. Unlike traditional geothermal, which relies on volcanic heat, next-generation geothermal could tap into underground heat in many more places.

Scientists are exploring three main types of advanced geothermal systems.

The first is Enhanced Geothermal Systems (EGS), which operate in areas without natural underground reservoirs by injecting water deep underground at high pressure to fracture rock and create artificial reservoirs. The heated water rises through another well, spins a turbine, and generates electricity in

a process similar to binary systems. The U.S. Department of Energy is testing EGS at sites like Newberry Volcano in Oregon and FORGE in Utah, with additional projects underway in Nevada, France, and Germany.

The next is Closed-loop geothermal systems (AGS), also called advanced geothermal systems, function like a car radiator. Rather than relying on underground water, these systems circulate a specialized heat-transfer fluid through sealed U-shaped pipes buried deep within the earth. The fluid absorbs heat, rises, cools at the surface, and recirculates, preventing groundwater contamination. However, AGS wells must extend at least five miles underground, significantly deeper than traditional geothermal wells. The first U.S. closed-loop demonstration was completed in 2022, with Germany planning a pilot project for 2028.

The last advanced system is called Superhot geothermal systems, which aim to reach extreme subterranean temperatures exceeding 750°F (400°C). These systems could integrate with existing methods—traditional, EGS, or AGS—while dramatically increasing energy production. However, no current technology is capable of handling such extreme conditions, at least not yet.

**One challenge with geothermal drilling is the small risk of triggering earthquakes, similar to what happens with fracking in the oil industry.**

One challenge with geothermal drilling is the small risk of triggering earthquakes, similar to what happens with fracking in the oil industry. Scientists such as Meier and Jelley say this risk is low but must be carefully managed. Otherwise, geothermal has very few environmental downsides. New binary power plants keep underground fluids contained, reducing pollution risks.

While solar and wind remain the most promising renewable energy sources, geothermal can be an important supplement. Fighting climate change requires many solutions, and geothermal energy has the potential to play a key role in that effort.

# Getting Real:

## PUMP UP THE JAM

Geothermal heat can work very well on a small scale too. Many homes in the United States use ground-source heat pumps for heating and cooling. Heat pumps have been around since the 1940s, boomed during the 1970s energy crisis, and are now the most popular geothermal technology in America. Heat pumps offer steady and even heating and cooling, take up less space that traditional combustion furnaces, don't require a chimney or vent, and don't create air pollutants. The heat-pump system collects heat from fluid-filled coils dug deep underground near the house. As the warm fluid reaches the heat pump, its collected heat energy goes through a heat exchanger which transfers it into the house. This warms the air inside the same way as a furnace or boiler, and can provide hot water on tap. During summers, the same process can work in reverse to cool the house, transferring the heat either back underground or into the air. Although it does require some electricity to run, it uses far less energy than a traditional gas or electric furnace because the heat is simply drawn from the existing reservoir underground. This can save a

lot of money on a monthly heating bill, though there is a bigger cost upfront to install the buried fluid coils. And ground-source pumps work very well in cold climates because the underground temperature is always fairly steady—and much warmer than a typical January day aboveground.

# A SONG OF ICE AND FIRE

Although larger nations like the U.S. and Indonesia produce more total geothermal power, no other nation has harnessed the volcano like Iceland. Settled by Vikings about 1,150 years ago, this tiny island outpost in the north Atlantic, halfway between Greenland and Europe, has a uniquely strong geothermal hook. It lies above a geologic "hot spot" where magma wells up from deep beneath the surface, and also

happens to be on the juncture between two dividing tectonic plates, the North American and Eurasian. This makes Iceland one of the most volcanically active places on Earth. That can be dangerous—more than 30 major eruptions have happened in the modern era, including the 1783 eruption of the volcano Laki which killed one-fifth of Iceland's population. But the people have also learned how to channel that awesome force into something positive.

Iceland made almost a third of its electricity from geothermal power in 2022. (And the rest came from hydropower, meaning that Iceland's electricity is 100% derived from clean, environmentally friendly sources.) The country has 35 geothermal plants in operation—the biggest is Krafla Geothermal Station, which produces 60 megawatts of power. There's potential for many more, given the 200 volcanoes and 600 hot springs dotting the island. But Iceland's greatest geothermal success may be its heating system, which provides warmth to 90 percent of the country's households. The cost savings provides a huge boost to the nation's economy. It also reduces their carbon emissions, a main cause of climate change, by an estimated 433 million tons. And it puts Iceland well in range of becoming the world's first nation to be completely free of fossil fuels.

# Timeline

**1904**

The first geothermal power experiment is conducted in Larderello, Italy, successfully producing electricity.

**1911**

Italy opens the world's first commercial geothermal power plant in Larderello, marking the start of industrial-scale geothermal energy.

**1960**

The first geothermal power plant in the U.S. begins operations at The Geysers in California.

**1973**

The oil crisis sparks renewed interest in geothermal energy as a stable alternative to fossil fuels.

**1976**

Iceland's Svartsengi Geothermal Power Plant is built, later leading to the creation of the Blue Lagoon.

**1998**

The Philippines becomes the world's second-largest producer of geothermal energy, surpassing the U.S. briefly.

**2006**

Nevada experiences a geothermal boom, with multiple plants opening in response to energy demand.

**2015**

Kenya expands geothermal capacity, becoming Africa's largest producer of geothermal electricity.

**2018**

The U.S. Department of Energy launches new research into enhanced geothermal systems (EGS) to unlock more geothermal potential.

**2023**

Iceland generates nearly 90% of its heating needs using geothermal energy, solidifying its leadership in geothermal technology.

# Websites

**Geothermal Rising**

*https://geothermal.org/*
Formed in 1972, this professional and educational association advocates for geothermal energy to the public.

**Frontier Observatory for Research in Geothermal Energy (FORGE)**

*https://www.energy.gov/eere/geothermal/forge*
Take a virtual tour of a next-generation geothermal project at this Department of Energy website.

**Earthships**

*https://theministryofarchitecture.com/earthships/*
Learn more about these experimental underground houses at the website of New Mexico's Ministry of Architecture.

# Glossary

**continental drift** —the movement of tectonic plates which builds new continents, and creates earthquakes and volcanoes

**fossil fuel** —hydrocarbon fuels such as petroleum oil and gas made in the ancient past from biological sources and found in Earth's crust

**fracking** —to fracture subterranean rock by injecting high-pressure water to ease oil or gas production

**geothermal** —relating to the heat of the interior Earth

**global warming** —a human-caused increase in worldwide air and ocean temperature

**greenhouse gas** — gases such as carbon dioxide, methane, and water vapor which contribute to global warming by absorbing infrared radiation (heat) and reflecting it back to Earth's surface

**pipeline** —a connected series of pipes for conveying a liquid or gas such as petroleum or steam

**plate tectonics** —in science, the concept that the Earth's crust is made up of plates which float on and move over the molten interior

**renewability** —a goal for alternative energy that it will never run out (such as sunlight and wind) or will replenish over time.

**sustainability** —a goal for alternative energy that it will not damage Earth's climate or humans' ability to harvest it.

**reservoir** —a large natural or manmade pool containing water or other liquids

# Selected Bibliography

"*A History of Geothermal Energy in America*", U.S. Department of Energy's Office of Energy Efficiency & Renewable Energy, 2013, https://web.archive.org/web/20230316014329/https://energy.gov/eere/geothermal/history-geothermal-energy-america

Berners-Lee, Mike. *There Is No Planet B: A Handbook for the Make Or Break Years*. United States, Cambridge University Press, 2019.

Jelley, Nick. *Renewable Energy: A Very Short Introduction*. United Kingdom, OUP Oxford, 2020.

McDonald, Bob. *The Future Is Now: Solving the Climate Crisis with Today's Technologies*. Canada, Penguin Canada, 2024.

Meier, Paul F., *The Changing Energy Mix: A Systematic Comparison of Renewable and Nonrenewable Energy* (New York, 2020; online edn, Oxford Academic, 18 Feb. 2021), https://doi-org.wikipedialibrary.idm.oclc.org/10.1093/oso/9780190098391.001.0001, accessed 29 Oct. 2024.

Rhodes, Richard. *Energy: A Human History*. United Kingdom: Simon & Schuster, 2019.

Simon, Christopher A.. Alternative Energy: Political, Economic, and Social Feasibility. United States, Rowman & Littlefield Publishers, 2020.

Usher, Bruce. Renewable Energy: A Primer for the Twenty-first Century. United States, Columbia University Press, 2019.

# Index